The Olympics

Anita Garmon

Contents

The Olympics Long Ago

Would you like to run a race wearing heavy armour? Would you play a game where the only rules were no biting and no eye poking? How would you feel if only the winner won a prize? Well, that's what the Olympic Games were like long ago.

The first Olympic Games took place in **ancient** Greece. They were held almost 3,000 years ago. The games honoured the god Zeus. He was the most powerful god in the ancient Greek religion. The Greeks held the games every four years.

A statue of Zeus holding an Olympic torch

People came from all over Greece to watch the games. Others came to be in the games. But only men could compete.

At first, there was just a short foot race. Soon, other sports, such as boxing and chariot racing, were added. One game was called pankration. It was a mix of boxing, wrestling and kicking. Players could do almost anything to win. There were only two rules. Players were not allowed to bite or to poke each other in the eyes.

Winners at the first games received crowns made from olive branches. The olive tree was very special in ancient Greece. There were no prizes for s[illegible]nd or third place.

Chariot racing

Olympic Traditions

Pierre de Coubertin, founder of the modern Olympics

When the Olympics are held, do you watch any of the events on TV? Have you seen the Olympic torch or the Olympic flag? Do you know the Olympic oath? What do these **traditions** mean?

The modern Olympics started in 1896. The people who started them hoped to promote peace and friendship around the world. Athletes from all nations would compete. The games would be held every four years in different cities.

The first modern Olympics was held in Athens, Greece. People wanted the new games to be like the ancient ones. So they did many of the same things that were done at the old games.

Olympic Symbols

The Olympic flame is the link between the modern and ancient games. It is lit in Olympia, Greece, the home of the first Olympics. A **relay** of runners carries the torch to the **site** of the games. Sometimes the runners carry the torch on foot. At other times, boats and planes carry the torch. The torch lights the main flame at the stadium. The flame burns throughout the games.

At the Sydney 2000 Olympic Games, the torch was taken underwater!

The Olympic flag flies during the games. The flag has five rings. Four rings stand for the **continents** of Africa, Asia, Australia and Europe. A fifth ring stands for the Americas (North America and South America). People from these continents play in the games. At the end of the games, the flag is given to the **host** of the next games.

The Opening Ceremonies

The opening ceremony is bright and colourful. The athletes parade around the stadium. They wave their country's flag. Greece is always first in the parade. Athletes from the other countries follow in alphabetical order. The host country is always last. The Olympic flag is raised and the flame is lit.

After the parade, one athlete and one judge take the Olympic oath. The oath says that the players will play by the rules and be good sports. This reminds us that the games must be fair and friendly.

Now, let the games begin!

Athletes march in the opening ceremony of the Sydney 2000 Olympic Games.

Meet the Athletes

Who competes in the Olympic games? How are these athletes chosen? What kind of training do they receive?

Each country chooses its Olympic team. Most of the athletes chosen are **amateurs**. This means that they are not paid money to play a sport. Each country pays for its team's uniforms, equipment and transportation to the games.

Athletes in some countries practise for the Olympics from the time they are children. These young athletes often live and train away from home. Despite years of training, not all of these athletes make it to the games.

This coach helps a gymnast train on the balance beam.

Coaches help athletes train for their events.

Athletes in many countries are invited to compete at **trials**. The trials are competitions to choose who will go to the Olympics. The athletes at the trials have all won other competitions. The winners of the trials then train for the Olympics. Many countries have special training camps for their athletes.

The Summer Games

Over 10,000 athletes compete in the Summer Olympics. These games take place in the summer season of the host country. There are almost 300 individual and team events. Contests are held in track and field, swimming, gymnastics, cycling and boxing. Many team games are also played at the Summer Games, including soccer, basketball and field hockey. Medals are given for first, second and third-place winners.

All the members of these winning cycling teams were given a medal.

Track and Field

Track and field is one of the most popular sports in the Summer Olympics. Track and field events include running, jumping and throwing. The shortest running race is 100 metres. The longest is the marathon, a race of about 42 kilometres.

In the long jump, athletes race down a runway and jump as far as they can into a sandpit. In the pole vault, they use a pole to jump over a high bar. The bar is raised until there is only one jumper who can leap over the bar.

Long jump

Swimming and Diving

There are many different swimming and diving events in the Summer Games. There are races and relays. There is platform diving. There is water polo. There is even synchronised swimming. In this event, people swim at the same time doing the same moves. Sometimes, these swimmers stay under water for over a minute. It is like running a race holding your breath!

Synchronised swimmers

A gymnast on a balance beam

Gymnastics

Are you a gymnast? Gymnastics is one of the most popular Olympic sports. There are many different kinds of gymnastic events. There are team and individual events. Athletes perform on balance beams, rings, bars, as well as on floor mats.

The Winter Games

Do you like the cold? Then you should try the Winter Games. Over 2,000 athletes compete in these games. All the Winter Games take place on snow or ice. There are more than 70 events in which players will win medals.

Skiing and Snowboarding

Skiing is a popular winter sport. There are many different skiing events. There are downhill races and cross-country races. There's also ski jumping.

Ski jumping

In this event, the skier races down a steep track and jumps off a platform at the end. There's also freestyle skiing where skiers perform different stunts on their skis. Maybe you like to snowboard. Snowboarding is like skateboarding on snow. This sport was added to the Olympics in 1998.

Ice-Skating

There are two types of ice-skating. One is speed skating. Skaters race on skates. They race individually and in teams. The second is figure skating. Skaters skate alone or in pairs. They skate to music. They spin, leap and move like acrobats on ice. Still another Olympic event is ice dancing. This is a mix of skating and ballroom dancing.

Speed skating

Sledding

Three sledding events are the luge, skeleton and bobsledding. The word *luge* means "sled" in French. In this event, racers lie on their backs and ride down an ice-covered track on small sleds.

In the skeleton, riders also compete on small sleds. However, they lie on their bellies and go down the track face first.

In bobsledding, teams of two or four sit inside a bobsled as they ride down the ice-covered track. In all three sledding events, the rider with the fastest time wins.

Luge

Ice hockey

Ice Hockey

Both men and women play ice hockey in the Olympics. Each team has six players. Ice hockey matches are fast and fun to watch.

People all around the world watch the Winter Games. But they watch it in their warm homes, not on a snow-capped mountain or in an ice arena.

Special Games

The Paralympics

The Paralympics are games for athletes with physical **disabilities**. The Paralympics hold Summer and Winter Games in the same city and year as the Olympics. The word *para* means that these games run beside the Olympics. Athletes compete in many of the same sports.

Paralympics opening ceremony

Wheelchair race

Winners receive gold, silver and bronze medals. Some of the medals have Braille written on them. This allows blind athletes to read their medals.

Some athletes race in wheelchairs. They race the same distances as in the Olympics. The athletes wear three layers of gloves when racing. This stops their hands from getting blisters.

The Special Olympics

Athletes with mental disabilities compete in the Special Olympics. Each year over a million athletes compete. The competitions are at world, regional, state and local levels.

Often, local schools and towns host the Special Olympics. Volunteers run the events. There are offices in many towns. If your town has one, you can help at this very special event.

This athlete has won many medals at the Special Olympics.

Glossary

amateur a person who is not paid money to participate in a sporting event

ancient very old; having existed long ago

continents the seven large landmasses on Earth—Africa, Antarctica, Asia, Australia, Europe, North America and South America

disability a physical or mental challenge that affects some people

host the city and country that holds the Olympic Games in a certain year

relay a race in which one runner passes an object, such as the Olympic torch, to another runner

site location, such as the city in which the Olympics are held

traditions activities that are performed over and over again as part of a ceremony

trials competitions that decide who will participate in an event

Index